The Little Golden
HYMNS

Compiled by
ELSA JANE WERNER and E.D. EBSUN

Illustrated by
FRANCES SCORE MITCHELL

A GOLDEN BOOK • NEW YORK
Western Publishing Company, Inc., Racine, Wisconsin 53404

Acknowledgments

The publishers wish to thank the following publishers and copyright owners for permission to use hymns in this book: Elizabeth McE. Shields for "A Prayer for Help" from *Worship and Conduct Songs*. Lorenz Publishing Co. for "Joy in Every Heart," copyright Tullar-Meredith Co. "Flowers Below and Stars Above" from *Religion-in-the-Kindergarten* by Bertha Marilda Rhodes; copyright 1924 by the University of Chicago; renewed 1951 by Bertha Marilda Rhodes; reprinted by permission of Harper & Row, Publishers, Inc. Words and music of "Evening Prayer" copyright 1935 by Presbyterian Board of Christian Education; renewed 1963; from *When the Little Child Wants to Sing*; reprinted by permission of The Westminster Press. The Pilgrim Press for "All Things Bright and Beautiful" from *Songs for Little People* by Danielson and Conant.

The publishers have made every effort to trace the ownership of all copyrighted material and to secure permission from the holders of such hymns. In the event of any question arising as to the use of any material, the publishers, while expressing regret for inadvertant error, will be pleased to make the necessary correction in future printings.

A Prayer for Help

Elizabeth McE. Shields

Claude T. Carr

Help us, Fa - ther, to re - mem - ber What you'd like to have us do;

Help us to be strong and lov - ing, Help us to be true.

This Is the Day

Psalms 118:24

Charles Cushing

This is the day which the Lord hath made;

We will re-joice_____ and be glad in it.

smoothly

broadening

The Creation

Words and Music by Johnie B. Wood

And God said the sun should shine, The
And God said the grass should grow, The

rain should fall, the flow'rs should grow, And God said the
trees bear fruit, the winds should blow, And God said the

birds should sing, And it was so, was so.
streams should flow, And it was so, was so.

All Things Bright and Beautiful

Cecil Frances Alexander

Danish Folk Song

Each lit - tle flower that o - pens, Each lit - tle bird that
The pur - ple - head - ed moun - tain, The riv - er run - ning
The cold winds in the win - ter, The pleas - ant sum - mer
He gave us eyes to see____ them, And lips that we might

sings, God made their glow - ing col - ors, He made their ti - ny wings.
by, The sun - set and the morn - ing red, That bright - en up the sky.
sun, The ripe fruits in the gar - den, He made them ev - 'ry one.
tell The good - ness of the Fa - ther, Who do - eth all things well.

To God Who Gives Us Daily Bread

M. Rumsey

Orlando Gibbons

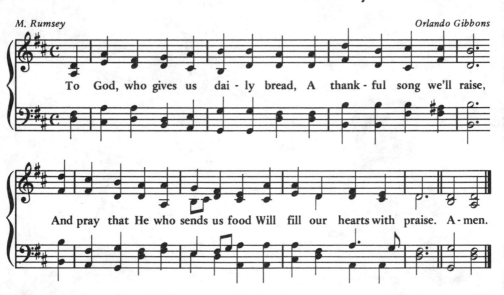

To God, who gives us dai - ly bread, A thank - ful song we'll raise,

And pray that He who sends us food Will fill our hearts with praise. A - men.

Joy in Every Heart

Mabel J. Rosemon

M. Isabelle Ritter

Songs of re - joic - ing fill the air, Ring-ing so sweet and clear.
All Na -ture joins the glo - ry song Ris - ing to heav'n to - day,
Come with re - joic - ing, one and all, Come with your pray'r and praise,

Bright -ness and glad - ness ev - 'ry-where Tell us that Sum-mer's here.
Each whis-p'ring breeze that sweeps a - long Bears hap - py notes a - way.
Pray'r that the Fa - ther's bless - ing fall, Praise for these tune-time days.

CHORUS

Joy, joy in ev-'ry heart With new life a-thrill,

Bright, bright the sun-beams glow, Hours with glo-ry fill;

Praise, praise the Lord a-bove, For these gold-en days.

Praise the Lord, O come and praise the Lord, And tell His won-drous ways.

Flowers Below and Stars Above

Bertha Marilda Rhodes

Old Folk Song

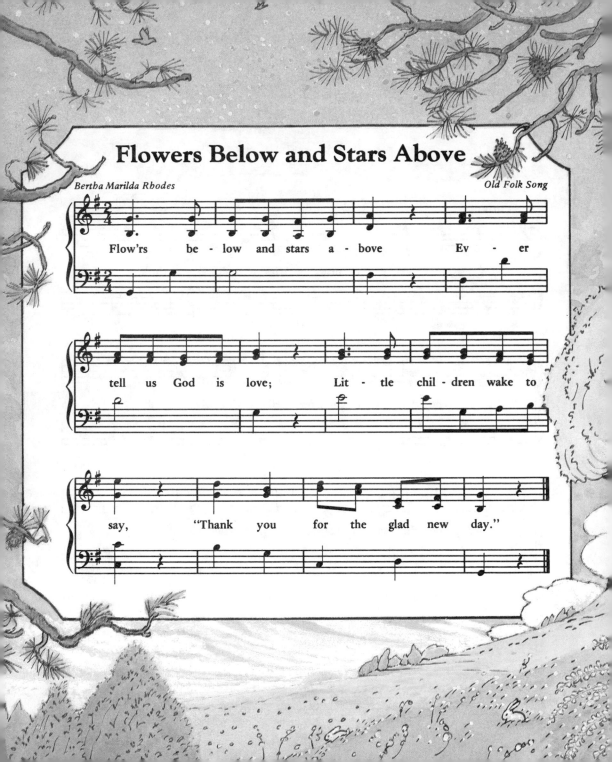

Flow'rs be - low and stars a - bove Ev - er
tell us God is love; Lit - tle chil - dren wake to
say, "Thank you for the glad new day."

Trust in God, Our Maker

George Wallace Briggs

Thomas Tallis

O God, by whom all things were made, Whose hand is o-ver all,
Thou mad-est all the stars in heav'n, The earth, the deep blue sea:
Thy wis-dom is too won-der-ful For me to un-der-stand:

Be-yond Thy care can no man stray, Nor can a spar-row fall.
Thou mad-est man to know Thy love, And so Thou mad-est me.
But this I know, in this I trust, That I am in Thy hand. A-men.

How Strong and Sure My Father's Care

Anonymous

Thomas Tallis

How strong and sure my Fa-ther's care, That 'round a-bout me, like the air,

Is with me al-ways, ev-'ry-where! He cares for me, He cares for me.

Away in a Manger

Words and Music by Martin Luther

A - way in a man - ger, No crib for a bed, The lit - tle Lord
The cat - tle are low - ing, The ba - by a - wakes, But lit - tle Lord

Je - sus Laid down His sweet head; The stars in the sky___ Looked
Je - sus, No cry - ing He makes. I love Thee, Lord Je - sus, Look

down where He lay, The lit - tle Lord Je - sus, A - sleep on the hay.
down from the sky, And stay by my cra - dle Till morn - ing is nigh.

Evening Prayer

Anonymous

Miriam Drury

Now I lay me down to sleep, I

pray Thee, Lord, Thy child to keep: Thy love guard me

through the night, And wake me with the morn - ing light.